The Ultimate
Drinking Games
Collection

Series Editor: Colleen Collier
Written and researched by: Sylvia Goulding
Contributors: Sue Curran
Page design & layout: Linley Clode
Cover Design: Gary Inwood Studios

Published by:

LAGOON BOOKS
PO Box 311, KT2 5QW, UK
PO Box 990676, Boston, MA 02199, USA

www.lagoongames.com

ISBN: 1-902813-31-6

Printed in Singapore.

THE ULTIMATE

DRINKING
GAMES

COLLECTION

LAGOON
BOOKS

— INTRODUCTION —

Whether you're with a large group of work colleagues, or simply having a quiet drink with a few close friends, you are guaranteed to have an unforgettable evening with this fabulous collection of drinking games.

Many of the games included need no extra props...just a great venue! However, some of them do require a few household items, so it may be worth checking out beforehand what you might need to make the night even more enjoyable.

Fill up those glasses, let your hair down, and be prepared to have the night of your life!

(Please note that these games have been assembled in a spirit of fun. We recommend that they are not played with alcoholic beverages. If they are played with alcohol, we urge players to exercise moderation in their alcohol consumption).

Section 1 ～ Bar Games

These are games that have been chosen to fit in with a fun social night in a bar. Some may require a few household items that have been brought along for the occasion, so make sure you check what may be needed before you leave the house!

Section 2 ～ Physical Games

These are games that need a bit of exertion and may cause a fair amount of embarrassment to the players! Be prepared to swallow your pride and make a fool of yourself – but don't worry, everyone else will have to as well!

Section 3 ～ Think & Drink

These games require some thought as well as action. Many are fast-paced and furious, and some even allow you to delve into the murky depths of your friends' minds! Train your brain and be prepared for some comic consequences!

Section 4 ～ Totally Outrageous

These games are probably best played toward the end of an evening, when you have got to know the other people in your party a bit better! They require no shame – only a healthy sense of humor! You have been warned!

INDEX

BAR
GAMES

– Law of Dice –

The dice must be obeyed – whatever they demand!

You will need four to 12 players, plus two dice.

The rules of this game are very simple – like in most good drinking games! – but they must be strictly adhered to.

All players sit in a circle and take turns throwing the dice. And here follows the Law of Dice:

(A) *Two – FINISH THE DRINK BELONGING TO THE PERSON ON YOUR RIGHT*

(B) *Three – LICK THE EAR OF YOUR NEIGHBOR (RIGHT OR LEFT!)*

(C) *Four – FINISH THE DRINK BELONGING TO THE PERSON ON YOUR LEFT*

(D) *Five – SWAP SHIRTS WITH YOUR NEIGHBOR (RIGHT OR LEFT!)*

(E) *Six – FINISH YOUR OWN DRINK*

(F) *Seven – ALLOW YOUR NEIGHBORS (RIGHT OR LEFT!) TO SPANK YOU*

(G) *Eight – THE PERSON ON YOUR RIGHT MUST FINISH YOUR DRINK*

(H) *Nine – EXPOSE YOUR MIDRIFF AND BELLY-DANCE ONCE AROUND THE TABLE*

(I) TEN – THE PERSON ON YOUR LEFT MUST FINISH YOUR DRINK

(J) ELEVEN – DO WHAT YOUR NEIGHBOR (RIGHT OR LEFT!) TELLS YOU TO DO FOR 60 SECONDS

(K) TWELVE – EVERYONE FINISHES THEIR DRINK AND YOU MUST BUY A NEW ROUND.

As you can see, there's some element of choice and, of course, you can devise your own rules for the game. But whatever you decide must be strictly obeyed.

— CHASE THE ACE —

Don't let it catch up with you!

You will need any amount of players,
and a deck of cards.

The aim of the game is to be left with a card of the highest possible value. Each player is dealt one card, which lies on the table face down. The first player to the left of the dealer looks at his card and decides whether to swap it with that of his neighbor who sits on his left. If he decides to swap, he has to accept the card he is given.

His neighbor now looks at his card, which may be either the one he had at the start or the one he's just received, and has to decide whether or not to swap it. And so the game continues.

If a player holds a King of any suit, he can refuse to swap – the King is the highest value card and is unbeatable. The person with the lowest card at the end of the round loses and has to finish his drink. Aces are low so they tend to be swapped around the table at alarming speed, usually ending up with the dealer! So make sure players take turns to be the dealer!

— LUMBER —

A game enjoyed not only by lumberjacks!

*You will need two to eight players,
a box of matches, and a bottle.*

Players take it in turns to place one matchstick at a time across the top of a bottle. The stack will become ever more precarious, and each addition will increase the risk of the entire structure tumbling down! When the pile finally does collapse, all players shout, *"LUMBER!"* and the player who caused the collapse has to finish the drink in front of him.

If the stack reaches a sizeable height, you could also turn this game into a form of 'Pick-a-stick', and players have to remove the matchsticks again from the bottle, using only the tips of their fingers, without making the heap collapse!

— Guzzle or Sink —

A relay game much loved by the owners of bars everywhere!

You will need two teams, each with at least four players, a referee, and a full drink for each player.

This game is a drinking relay where speed is of the essence! Choose two team leaders who will, alternately, pick their team-mates. This is important – for some people obviously have greater reputations as 'guzzlers' than others do! Line up the two teams next to each other.

The referee says the word *"Go"*, and the first players in the two teams start drinking their beverage as fast as they can. As soon as they've finished their drink, they place the empty glass on their head. This is the signal for the next team member to start drinking.

The winning team is the one that finishes first – and it is only fair they should buy a round of drinks for the losers!

— GRANDMA'S FOOTSTEPS —

Who will win the race to the bar – and the next drink?

You will need any amount of players, a player to be the 'grandmother', and plenty of space in a bar!

This child's game – also known as 'Statues' – is great fun when played in a bar with drinks as prizes. One person is chosen to be the 'grandmother', and he will prop up the bar with his own drink.

All the other players, meanwhile, are lined up at the opposite side of the room. On the word *"Go"*, players will start to creep towards the bar without 'grandmother' noticing. 'Grandmother', naturally suspicious, will occasionally turn around at which time all players need to freeze on the spot in whatever position they happen to be in – one foot in mid-air, one arm stretched forward, and so on.

Everyone caught moving by 'grandmother' will have to leave the race and wait until the next round before they can have a drink. Everyone who reaches the bar 'unnoticed' can down a drink and the first person to reach it will be bought a drink by 'grandmother'.

– Nose Race –

A slow and furious – well, infuriating! – race!

You will need two teams of players, a referee, a 'Start' and 'Finish' line (about ten feet apart) and a pea for each team.

Races of any kind are a typical bar pursuit, and this is a race where a large nose could be a definite advantage!

The objective of the game is very simple – a single pea has to be pushed from the 'Start' to the 'Finish' line and back by every player in the teams as a relay race. In order to chase the pea, players have to get on their hands and knees and push it with their noses. Other team members will obviously wish to shout their encouragement, but they are not allowed to interfere.

The referee needs to ensure that no player uses their hands or any part of their body other than their noses. Each transgression is to be paid for by a drinking penalty (see p.46 for ideas). The losing team has to buy a round of drinks for the winning team – and, of course, they may wish to challenge them to a replay!

— HOMER SAYS... —

The world's favorite TV family decides your actions!

You will need any amount of players, a TV screen showing an episode of 'The Simpsons' in a bar.

This is one of those wonderful drinking games that allows you to watch TV at the same time, and you don't even have to talk to your fellow bar-mates. Indeed, you could play the game entirely on your own if you were so inclined.

The rules are astonishingly simple. Just watch 'The Simpsons' and see what the characters do or say. Here's how to translate their actions into yours:

(A) HOMER SAYS "DOH" – DRINK TWO FINGERS OF YOUR DRINK

(B) MARGE GRUMBLES – BUY THE BARMAN A DRINK

(C) BART IS RUDE – DRINK FOUR FINGERS OF YOUR DRINK

(D) LISA SAYS SOMETHING INTELLIGENT – KISS YOUR NEIGHBOR'S HAND

(E) KRUSTY THE KLOWN APPEARS – FINISH YOUR DRINK

(F) THE CHILDREN WATCH VIOLENCE ON TV – BUY ANOTHER DRINK

(G) HOMER IS EATING – BUY A 'CHASER' FOR SOMEONE ELSE

(H) THE FAMILY ARE ALL EATING TOGETHER – DRINK A 'CHASER'

(I) 'ITCHY & SCRATCHY' ARE ON TELEVISION – BUY A DRINK FOR SOMEONE AT ANOTHER TABLE

(l) *APOO MAKES A SALE — GO TO THE BATHROOM*

(k) *THE HEADMASTER SCOLDS BART — SAY "I LOVE YOU" TO THE*
     PERSON SEATED ON YOUR LEFT

(l) *MAGGIE SUCKS HER PACIFIER — DRINK A GLASS OF MILK.*

Make up your own list of commands if you prefer, and appoint a referee to ensure that all commands are strictly adhered to.

— KING OF THE BAR —

*A great warm-up game to play
in a bar or restaurant.*

*You will need any amount of players,
plus a deck of cards.*

Simplicity is the name of this game. You don't have to calculate, plan, remember any rules, or think – all you have to do is drink!

The dealer shuffles a deck of cards, and deals them out one at a time to each player face up. The cards lie on the table in full view of all the other players. The dealer carries on dealing one card to each player until the first King appears.

The player who is dealt the first King names his favorite long drink. The dealer continues until the second King appears, and the player who receives it names his favorite 'chaser'. The dealer continues again until the third King appears, and the player who receives it has to buy the long drink and the 'chaser'. The dealer continues until the fourth King is dealt out, and the lucky person who receives this card has to drink them!

15

— BEER ROULETTE —

Lady Luck devised this bar game which may put you under the table in no time!

You will need any amount of players, a croupier, plus one die per player.

Each player is issued with a die and on the word, *"ROLL"*, all players roll their dice simultaneously, as if in a synchronized dice-rolling display. At the same time, the croupier – who also rolls his die – shouts out either *"EVEN"* or *"ODD"*, or a number between one and six.

Anyone whose die total fits into the 'Even' or 'Odd' category that has been chosen has to take a gulp of his drink. Anyone whose die shows the exact number that has been called 'wins' double – he has to finish his drink. This does, of course, include the croupier himself and he'll need to be strictly watched to ensure that he doesn't call when he already knows what his own die says!

— BLIND HUGHIE —

A fast, fun dominoes game without the need for strategies.

You will need two to five players, a set of dominoes, a large table, plus a pen and paper for the scores.

Shuffle all the domino tiles. Each player picks one tile, and the highest accumulated score starts. Replace all the tiles and shuffle them again. Deal them all out (not dealing one of the dominoes at the end if there are three players, and not dealing three of the dominoes at the end if there are five players).

Players arrange their tiles face down, in a row in front of them. The player to the left of the dealer starts, or else a leftover tile is placed face up in the middle. The player picks up his first tile and places it if he can – equal numbers adjoining in the same line, or a tile with doubles adjoining horizontally.

Play goes around the table with each player picking up their first tile and trying to place it. If their tile doesn't fit, they replace it at the end of the line of their tiles, face down again. If it is a double that doesn't fit, they also replace this at the end, but face up this time.

Play goes round and round, with the players all trying to get rid of their tiles. The first player to do so shouts *"DOMINOES"* and wins the round. If the game is blocked and no player can go, the remaining domino values are counted up and the player with the lowest value wins, scoring the difference between his own and that of the next highest score.

While the game is going on, the following rules apply:

(A) *EVERY PLACEMENT MEANS DRINK A FINGER OF YOUR DRINK*

(B) *EVERY DOUBLE PLACEMENT MEANS DRINK TWO FINGERS OF YOUR DRINK*

(C) *EVERY LACK OF A PLACEMENT MEANS FINISH YOUR DRINK*

(D) *THE SHOUT OF "DOMINOES" MEANS BUY THE NEXT ROUND!*

PHYSICAL GAMES

— LEFT OR RIGHT? —

You'll need to be able to count to ten and know your right from your left for this game – not as easy as it sounds!

You will need any amount of players.

Player One determines the direction of play by placing a hand on his chest. If he places his right hand on the left side of his chest, play goes to the left. If he places his left hand on the right side of his chest, play goes to the right.

The next player is free to either repeat the previous action, continuing in the same direction, or to change direction. And so the game continues, until it reaches Player Five who has to place both hands on top of each other in the middle of his chest, the direction of play being indicated by the direction in which the fingers of his topmost hand are pointing. Player Ten, when he is reached, just points at any other player who instantly has to take up the game and indicate a direction, and so on.

This may sound quite simple, but a high degree of concentration is not what most people tend to possess after a few drinks, so much laughter, hesitation, challenges and complaints will ensue – all of which call for drinking penalties (see p.46 for ideas)!

— DRINK FOR DOLLARS —

This game allows you to drink in order to get rich quick!

You will need any amount of players, all with pockets holding lots of quarters, plus a pitcher of your chosen beverage.

You may think it odd to pay for your drink twice, but this is – potentially – a great way to replenish dwindling funds! Players sit in a circle and pass the pitcher around to the left. The first player must drop a quarter into the pitcher that then entitles him to drink as much as he wishes. When he's had enough (for the moment), he passes the pitcher to the left, and now the second player has to pay and drink.

At any one point, whoever holds the pitcher may decide to take all the money that's accumulated within it, and he's allowed to do so – as long as he finishes all the drink that's left in the pitcher!

You'll soon understand the strategy needed behind this game of high finance – if you're not intending to gain the entire fund, you'll just take a sip in the hope that there'll

be too much left in the pitcher for the next person to guzzle it all. When you see the number of quarters building up in the bottom of the jug, however, you may suddenly decide to go for it and finish the lot and pocket the fund.

It's only fair on other players, though, that the winner buys the next pitcher!

— CRABS —

***You don't have to run sideways,
but you do have to run fast!***

*You will need two teams of at least four players each,
a bartender, a table holding a pitcher of your
chosen beverage, and one glass per team.*

This is a team relay race, so allow two players to alternately pick the members of their team. The teams assemble on one side of the room, the bartender and the table with the glasses and the drink are at the other side of the room. The first player in each team sits down, puts their hands behind them on the floor and lifts their bottom off the floor to allow them to walk around like a crab!

On the word *"Go"*, the two players race toward the table where they are each issued with a full glass from the bartender that is then placed between their thighs. Then the players race back to their teams, where the second player takes the glass, drinks a hefty amount (preferably emptying it), and then it is his turn to assume the crab position, and place the empty glass between his own thighs to race back to the table for a refill.

Bonus points are awarded for each glass that is emptied rather than just sipped from, and five points go to the team that finishes first. The team with the highest total of points chooses the next game – and the team with the lowest number of points pays a drinking penalty each (see p.46 for ideas)!

— High Noon —

A liquid version of the shoot-out at the OK Corral which may leave you just as 'dead'.

You will need two to ten players, plenty of canned drinks per player, plus a high-velocity water pistol for each player!

This shoot-out can take place anywhere, but preferably outside on a hot and sunny day. In fact, the very best place to play is on the beach!

All players stand in a circle, about 30 to 40 feet apart from each other, and each one is given a drinks can and a water pistol gun. Players place the cans in front of their feet.

On *"Fire"*, each player is given ten seconds to try and shoot over one of the other players' cans. Any can that is toppled over will need to be drunk and replenished with a new can. The loser will also need to move one step towards the center of the circle. This continues, until players come face-to-face, in which case they start moving outwards again.

This game is particularly effective if several players gang up on one person, perhaps in several consecutive rounds. Their combined firepower will ensure that the can is toppled over and, after a few rounds, so will the hapless loser!

The same game can also be played with baseballs, tennis balls or Frisbees instead of water pistols.

— 'Gators in the Bayou —

A snappy game that's perfect for hot summer days!
You will need any amount of players,
plus a long piece of string.

Play this game in the garden or in a large room. Lay out string to outline the bayou and choose a player to be the 'gator who lives there. All the other players are to be Cajuns and have to keep on crossing the bayou while the 'gator tries to snap at them. If you have a swimming pool, so much the better – it'll be a far more realistic bayou!

Every Cajun who's gobbled up, ie touched, by the 'gator has to finish his drink and then become part of the 'gator's body, holding on to its waist and also snapping at the remaining intrepid Cajuns.

The last Cajun to outwit the 'gator is obviously far too smart and has to down three drinks in a row to bring him down to the level of the rest of the gang!

— $\mathcal{S}$IXTY $\mathcal{S}$ECOND $\mathcal{S}$HUFFLE —

***Don't worry, in this game you won't be
forced to talk non-stop – it's much worse!***

*You will need any amount of players, a referee,
a room or a 'Finish' line, plus a stopwatch.*

Cover, hide or confiscate all watches, video clocks or
other timepieces. On the word *"Go"*, the stopwatch
starts and all players sit down and start shuffling on their
bottoms towards the other side of the room (or the 'Finish'
line). The difficult part is that players must arrive at the
'Finish' line after exactly 60 seconds, not too early and
not too late! They are also not allowed to stop anywhere,
but constantly have to be on the move.

Any player who stops during the 60 seconds is
immediately eliminated and has to take a drink. Any
player who reaches the 'Finish' line before the 60
seconds are over, is also eliminated and has to take a
drink. When the 60 seconds are finished, the referee

shouts *"FREEZE"*, and players have to stop exactly where they are. The person closest to the 'Finish' line is the winner. For all the others, the distance from their bottom to the 'Finish' line is measured in feet and they have to consume one drink per foot!

– Blow Your Top –

I'll huff and I'll puff, and I'll blow the house down!

*You will need any amount of players,
a bottle, and a deck of cards.*

Place a deck of cards on top of a bottle. Players have to take turns to try and blow the top card off the pack. (This is easier if the cards are fairly new, as they will still be shiny and varnished). You could also play this game with beer mats instead of cards.

If more than one card is blown off, the player has to drink as many fingers of his drink as there are extra cards.
If the entire pack goes, the player has to finish his entire drink. If a player doesn't succeed in blowing any cards off the bottle, he has to buy the next round.

— GRAND SLAM —

A boisterous game where luck and speed are of the essence.

You will need four to 13 players, a deck of cards, and some small objects that number one less than the number of participating players (coins or matches).

Prepare the cards so that each player has four cards of a kind (for example, four tens, four Kings, etc). All players sit around a table, and in the center of the table the small objects are arranged. (If you're feeling really vicious, you could use eggs – all hard-boiled bar one that is still raw!)

The dealer shuffles the cards and deals them out face down. Players look at their cards and, on a given signal, everyone pushes one card they do not want to the player on their left. Everyone now looks at their new card and decides whether to pass it on or keep it, while passing on one more from their hand.

The game continues until one of the players has a set of four cards, in which case he has to slam them down on the table and shout *"SLAM!"*. On this signal, everyone grabs one of the small objects from the table, leaving one person without – the loser, who will have to down a drink before rejoining the game.

— Sweet Tooth —

If you're onto your third set of teeth,
this game will be a piece of pie!

You will need any amount of players.

Each player has to choose a dessert, for example, Key Lime Pie, Death by Chocolate, Shoofly Pie, Chocolate Chip Cookies, Bananas Foster, Banoffi Pie, etc. The longer the name, the better. All players take it in turn to say what their chosen dessert is, and then the game begins.

The first person calls out the name of their dessert followed by that of another person's dessert, and that player must repeat his own dessert followed by that of yet another person, and so on. All this has to happen at great speed, but there's also one extra hindrance – players must talk without their teeth showing (as they have obviously lost them due to overindulgence in sweet things)!

Any glimpse of tooth is punished with a drinking forfeit (see p.46), and any laughter (however subdued) calls for a major drinking penalty. Similarly, incoherent speech – whether caused by missing teeth or as a consequence of drinking forfeits – will also be severely punished.

— REVERSE COUNTDOWN —

This game will severely test
the speed of your reactions.

You will need any amount of players.

This game can be played at any point during a soirée or party. At any time during the evening, a player sits down on a chair and shouts *"ONE"*. This has to be immediately followed by another player shouting *"TWO"* and sitting down, the next one shouting *"THREE"*, etc. The last person to have sat down and shouted out their relevant number then has to finish all of his drink!

The trouble is that everyone will be shouting a number at the same time and when this happens, all these players are disqualified and have to finish their drink too!

— MY BUDDY —

***Camaraderie and friendship will be
severely tested by this game!***

*You will need any amount of players,
a ball, plus a stopwatch.*

Player One starts by throwing the ball at one of the other players and announcing *"THIS IS MY BUDDY"*, upon which the 'buddy' has to burst into song declaring his love or friendship, for example, *'I WILL ALWAYS LOVE YOU'* or *'YOU ARE THE SUNSHINE OF MY LIFE'*. The buddy needs to start singing within ten seconds of receiving the ball, and he cannot use a song that has been used before.

After singing the first line or so – more could seriously threaten any friendship! – Buddy throws the ball to another player, who has to continue with another song, again within ten seconds. Instead of using the stopwatch, all other players can loudly count which is very off-putting.

Any buddy can always reverse the game by singing a song about going it alone, such as *'I WILL SURVIVE'*, and returning the ball to the player who has just thrown it.

Any hesitations, duplicated songs, or wrong tunes will be punished by a drinking forfeit (see p.46).

— THE ART OF DARTS —

*A game for world champions and
absolute beginners alike.*

*You will need any amount of players,
plus a dartboard and darts.*

Form two teams. Each player has just one dart throw at a time, and what he throws determines what action he must take. Even throws beyond the board are not 'lost' in this game. Here follow some sample rules (which you can adapt as you wish):

(A) BLACK AREA — GIVE DETAILS OF YOUR MOST RECENT KISS

(B) WHITE AREA — MAKE UP A POEM ABOUT ONE PART OF
YOUR BODY

(C) DOUBLES — DRINK A DOUBLE 'CHASER'

(D) DOUBLE 13 — ADMIT WHO AMONG THE PLAYERS YOU
MOST FANCY

(E) TRIPLES — ALLOW THREE PLAYERS TO DROP AN ICE-CUBE DOWN
YOUR SHIRT OR PANTS

(F) TRIPLE 20 — NOMINATE ANOTHER PLAYER TO FINISH THEIR DRINK

(G) BULLS EYE — EVERYONE BUYS YOU A DRINK

(H) BEYOND THE BOARD — FINISH YOUR DRINK.

45

— **F**ORFEITS —

(A) STAND ON A TABLE AS STILL AS A STATUE FOR FIVE MINUTES

(B) SIT ON THE KNEE OF THE PLAYER THAT YOU FANCY THE MOST

(C) WALK ACROSS THE ROOM ON HANDS AND FEET (NOT KNEES), BALANCING A BAG ON YOUR BOTTOM

(D) ALLOW EVERY OTHER PLAYER TO TICKLE YOU WITHOUT LAUGHING

(E) SING 'THERE'S NO BUSINESS LIKE SHOW BUSINESS' AT THE TOP OF YOUR VOICE

(F) DRINK A PINT OF WATER DOWN IN ONE

(G) FINISH THE DRINK OF THE PERSON OPPOSITE YOU

(H) GET DOWN ON YOUR KNEES AND PROPOSE TO THE PERSON ON YOUR LEFT

(I) GARGLE TO THE TUNE OF 'I'M DREAMING OF A WHITE CHRISTMAS'

(J) DON'T TOUCH YOUR OWN DRINK FOR TEN MINUSTES

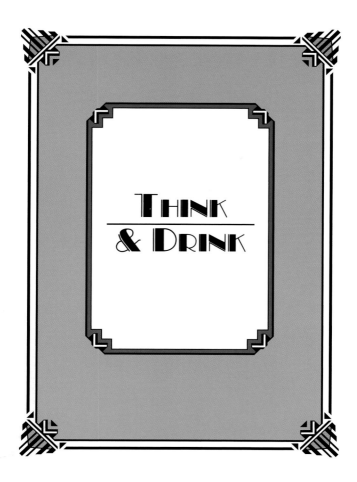

THINK
& DRINK

— REVEAL THE TRUTH —

A game of dilemmas may be the last thing you want to play after a few drinks!

You will need any amount of players, a referee, pens and paper, plus paper cut into playing card-sized pieces.

Players sit in a circle and each one writes down three different dilemmas on three seperate pieces of card, and then places his cards upside down in the center of the table. The cards are then shuffled and dealt back out to players – one each.

Each player now has three dilemmas in front of him from various other players. He has to guess what the neighbor on his left would choose to do, and writes this down secretly on a piece of paper. He then passes the choices to his neighbor, who has to write down his actual choices.

When the referee shouts, *"REVEAL THE TRUTH"*, neighbors compare their choices – what each thought the other might choose and what he actually did choose. Every correct guess brings a point, every incorrect guess means that you have to drink a finger from your glass.

At the end of the number of rounds you decide on, the player with the highest number of points wins.

Here are some sample dilemmas:
Would you rather…

(A) LOOK LIKE A FISH, OR SMELL LIKE A FISH?

(B) HAVE YOUR EYES ON THE ENDS OF YOUR INDEX FINGERS, OR
HAVE YOUR EYES IN THE BACK OF YOUR HEAD?

(C) SWEAT GARLIC BUTTER, OR CRY PORRIDGE?

(D) HAVE REALLY BAD BREATH, OR EVERYONE YOU MEET
HAVE REALLY BAD BREATH?

(E) HAVE HOLOGRAPHIC EYEBALLS, OR HAVE GLOW-IN-THE-DARK HAIR?

53

— CENTIPEDE —

A game of many legs!

You will need any amount of players, pens and paper for each player, plus a stopwatch.

This may seem to be a fairly mindless sort of game, but you'll be surprised at how quickly your mind will go blank!

Pick a letter from the alphabet. This can be done by one person silently saying the alphabet to themselves, and then being stopped by a second person. The letter they've reached is the one for the first round of the game.

All players have ten minutes to try to think of as many things with legs that start with the same letter and write them down. If the letter was B, for example, this could include Bus driver, Beggar, Businessman, Budgie, Boy, Bogart, etc. Names of famous people are allowed as long as everyone knows them.

When the time is up, compare notes. All entries that are wrong by consent, for example, legless items such as Bananas, are instantly punished by a drinking forfeit (see p.46). Cross out all the legged things that more than one person have mentioned, and award a point for each one that is totally unique. At the end of each round, the person with the highest number of points has to have a drink.

One consolation if you only had two or three entries – after a few rounds, the previous winners will have had lots to drink and won't be able to think of more than one or two entries either!

— GRANAMAS —

No, this isn't a misspelling!

You will need any amount of players,
plus pens and paper for each player.

Anagrams (yes, that's where the title comes from!) is an old family favorite, and can occupy players for hours. Yet after a few drinks, these will become increasingly difficult to fathom out.

Agree on a number of categories (say five). These could include things like flowers, TV soaps, vacation resorts, or cocktails, for example. Each player now has ten minutes to try to think of as many anagrams as they can within each category.

When the time is over, lists are compared. Should two players have worked out the same anagram – which does happen! – they have to pay a drinking forfeit (see p.46). The rest are all voted on to decide the best in each category, and awarded a point each.

At the end of the game, all high scorers have to buy a drink for all low scorers – as a consolation prize and punishment, all in one!

— WALLOP —

A quick mind – and nerves of steel – should steer you through this game.

You will need any amount of players.

Decide on a category – anything from car makes to female film stars who don't have breast implants! The first player has to think of someone or something belonging to this category and start describing him, her or it to everyone else.

As soon as a player thinks he has guessed the person or thing in question, he shouts *"WALLOP!"* – **not** the name of the person or thing! If the name slips out, a drink must be taken. Game then passes to the player who shouted, *"WALLOP"* first, and he either describes another person or thing within the same category, or sets a new category.

If anyone doubts that the secret guess is correct, they can challenge. If the challenger is right and the 'Walloper' guesses incorrectly, the 'Walloper' has to take a drink; if the challenger is wrong and the 'Walloper' does know the right answer, he has to take a drink instead.

— ❚NQUISITION —

Secrets will always come out!

You will need any amount of players, plus a spotlight or desk lamp that can be aimed at the person to be questioned.

The simple rule of this game is that one player asks another player a question, and this question can only ever be answered with *"YES"* or *"NO"*. Get into the right frame of mind by turning off all lights, apart from a single 'spotlight' that is aimed at the main player. Obviously, all questions need to be 'Yes/No' questions. If a player asks, *"DO YOU PREFER BEER TO WINE?"*, that is a question that cannot be answered with *"YES"* or *"NO"*, and they will have to pay a drinking penalty (see p.46).

The trick of this game is to come up with hugely embarrassing questions, the sort that cannot be answered lightly one way or the other, for example, *"IS THERE ANYONE IN THIS ROOM YOU'D LIKE TO KISS PASSIONATELY?"*

Questions need to be literally 'fired' at the victim, and they need to be answered immediately and countered by

a return question as soon as possible. Any waiting time or hesitation in answering is to be severely punished with a drinking penalty.

In order to increase speed, it's useful to intersperse personal questions with straightforward ones, such as *"IS YOUR NAME JERRY?"* or *"ARE YOU ENJOYING THIS GAME?"*

— TOTAL RECALL —

**Thirsty friends and a good memory
blend well in this game.**

You will need any amount of players.

This game can, of course, be played in a bar, but can just as easily be played at home.

All the players sit around a table, and the first player starts by saying, *"KIM (THE SPEAKER'S NAME) WENT TO THE BAR AND BOUGHT A SHOT OF RUM FOR SPIKE"*. One after the other, all the players repeat this phrase and the last one adds, *"…AND SAID 'KEEP THE CHANGE'"*.

In the next round, another order is added by the next player, for example, *"KIM WENT TO THE BAR AND BOUGHT A SHOT OF RUM FOR SPIKE, AND A BOTTLE OF BEER FOR JEFF"*. Again everyone repeats this, and so the game continues until someone fluffs his order. In which case, they should buy a round or pay a drinking forfeit (see p.46).

— Talk Sense —

Have a think, or sink that drink!
You will need any amount of players.

This word game is quite straightforward, although not as easy as it initially sounds. The objective is to form ever-lengthening sentences, but somehow never quite complete them.

Player One starts by saying a word, any word, for example *"SUNSHINE"* or *"ALCOHOL"*. Player Two then adds a word that fits grammatically and could potentially make a sentence. So to follow *"SUNSHINE"*, he might add *"WARMS"*. Player Three then adds another word, for example, *"THE"*, and so on.

Penalties will be imposed for the following misdemeanours:

> (A) *ADDING A WORD THAT DOESN'T FIT, FOR EXAMPLE, "WINTER" AFTER "SUNSHINE" — DRINK A FINGER OF YOUR DRINK*
>
> (B) *USING A THIRD ADJECTIVE IN A ROW — DRINK TWO FINGERS OF YOUR DRINK*

Another player starts off the next round, and on it goes.

– DRINKS R US –

Degrees of subtlety come into force during this game.

You will need any amount of players,
plus pens and paper for each player.

All players write down five drinks they like and five drinks they don't like. Then they fold up their papers and place them in a pile. One player picks up a piece of paper at a time, one at a time, and everyone else has to guess whose list it is. The sooner the person is guessed correctly, the higher the drinking penalty they will have to pay, as they are obviously far too predictable (see p.46).

The nuances and variations in this game depend on how well all the players know each other, and therefore how much you give away in your lists. Do you, for example, just say that you're fond of rosé wine, or do you mention a specific Californian Zinfandel?

TOTALLY
OUTRAGEOUS

— UNDERPANTS ON HEAD —

*Well, if you must insist on showing
everyone your underwear…*

*You will need any amount of players,
two dice, plus a clean pair of underpants.*

Players sit in a circle and take it in turns to roll the dice. Depending on the numbers a player rolls, he must take one of the following actions:

(A) TWO – THE ROLLER TAKES A DRINK

(B) THREE – THE PERSON TO THE LEFT OF THE ROLLER TAKES A DRINK

(C) FOUR – TEN SECONDS OF ABSOLUTE SILENCE – ANYONE WHO TALKS OR GIGGLES HAS TO TAKE A DRINK

(D) FIVE – EVERYONE HAS TO TAKE A DRINK

(E) SIX – EVERYONE HAS TO BOW TO THE ROLLER AND SAY, "LONG LIVE HIS MAJESTY!" – ANYONE WHO FORGETS HAS TO TAKE A DRINK

(F) SEVEN – EVERYONE HAS TO SIT ON THEIR HANDS – THE LAST PERSON TO DO SO TAKES A DRINK

(G) EIGHT – THE ROLLER NOMINATES ANOTHER PLAYER TO TAKE A DRINK

(H) NINE – THE PERSON TO THE RIGHT OF THE ROLLER
     TAKES A DRINK

(I) TEN – PLAYERS MAY INTERRUPT TO GO FOR A BATHROOM
     BREAK (FORBIDDEN AT ALL OTHER TIMES)

(J) ELEVEN – UNDERPANTS ON HEAD!

(K) TWELVE – UNDERPANTS ON HEAD!

When the numbers 11 or 12 are rolled, the player has to take the underpants and put them on his head. As if this wasn't degrading enough, they then have to carry on playing whilst wearing them! On no account can they be taken off, until someone else rolls an 11 or 12.

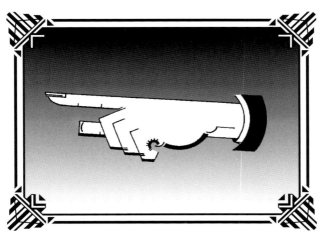

— Royal Salutes —

A fast card game for a late-night session.

*You will need any amount of players,
one or two decks of cards (depending on the
number of players), plus a table.*

This game is also known as 'Good Morning, Madam'
but, in our case, we're not talking about mornings and
the salutes are rather different! The players all sit around a
table and the cards are dealt out to them, face down.
Players are not allowed to look at their cards. The player
to the left of the dealer starts and places one card in the
center of the table, face up. The person to his left lays
one on top face up also, and so on, around the table.

As soon as the Ace, King, Queen or Jack are turned over,
all players try to be the first to do the following
commands:

> (A) ACE – SLAM YOUR HAND ON TOP OF THE CARD
>
> (B) KING – DOWN YOUR DRINK IN ONE
>
> (C) QUEEN – LOUDLY SHOUT "ANOTHER DRINK, PLEASE", AND
> THEN DRAIN YOUR GLASS
>
> (D) JACK – SHOW EVERYONE YOUR TUMMY BUTTON!

The first person to take the appropriate action wins all the cards in the pile. The aim is to collect all the cards that have been dealt. This player is declared the winner and everyone else has to pay a drinking forfeit! (see p.46)

— COCKTAIL BAR —

It's always said that you shouldn't mix your drinks – but how do you make a cocktail without mixing them?

You will need two to six players, plus pre-prepared 'Cocktail' cards.

Prepare a set of 'Cocktail' cards as follows:

(A) TEN 'FROZEN MARGARITA' CARDS, EACH WITH A SUCCESSIVE ALCOHOL CONTENT OF 10, 20, 30…UP TO 100 PER CENT

(B) TEN 'BOURBON SIDECAR' CARDS, EACH WITH A SUCCESSIVE ALCOHOL CONTENT OF 10, 20, 30…UP TO 100 PER CENT

(C) TEN 'MINT JULEP' CARDS, EACH WITH A SUCCESSIVE ALCOHOL CONTENT OF 10, 20, 30…UP TO 100 PER CENT

(D) TEN 'EYE OF THE HURRICANE' CARDS, EACH WITH A SUCCESSIVE ALCOHOL CONTENT OF 10, 20, 30…UP TO 100 PER CENT

(E) FOUR 'DOWN IN ONE' CARDS

(F) FOUR 'KISS THE BARTENDER' CARDS

(G) FOUR 'SWAP' CARDS.

The aim of this game is to get rid of all your cards as quickly as possible. Deal seven cards to each player (or five if more than four people are playing). Players take up their cards and look at them. The rest of the cards are placed, face down, in the center of the table with the top card turned face up beside the stockpile.

The first player needs to place the same cocktail, or another cocktail of the same alcohol content, on top of the turned over card. For example, if the top card is a 'Bourbon Sidecar' with an alcohol content of 50 per cent, he can place another 'Bourbon Sidecar' card of any other alcohol content on top, or else a different cocktail card that also has an alcohol content of 50 per cent.

If a player can't go, he needs to pick another card from the stockpile – and take a swig of his own drink straight away.

You are allowed to play the special cards at any time. The 'Down in One' cards mean that everyone has to finish their drink in one go, and the player to the left of the person who placed the card has to pick up three extra cards from the stockpile.

The 'Kiss the Bartender' cards mean exactly that – kiss the bartender or, if you're playing at home, the host. This probably means you!

The 'Swap' cards mean you have to swap an item of clothing with one other player, as well as swap drinks with the same person and drain their glass. It also allows you to put down any card and change the type of cocktail on the top.

The player who gets rid of all his cards first has to be bought a drink by the player left with the most cards!

— SPIN AND SWAP —

**Watch where the bottle points
– you could lose your pants!**

*You will need any amount of players,
plus a bottle (preferably empty).*

Everyone sits in a circle and in the center of the table, the bottle is spun. The first player it points to when it stops spinning has to take a drink. It is then spun again, and the second player it points to also has to take a drink. In addition, Player One and Player Two have to exchange one item of clothing (it doesn't necessarily have to be the same piece).

The bottle is now spun again, and the next two players follow the same routine. Players are not allowed to swap an item of clothing that they have received from someone else though! During the course of the game, players will end up wearing less of their own clothes and more of everyone else's – with hilarious results!

— THE JUG GAME —

Lack of judgement could be costly in this game!

You will need any amount of players, plus a large pitcher of a chosen beverage.

The pitcher of drink is passed around the table and each player drinks as little or as much as they wish. The only rule that applies is that the person who takes the penultimate drink has to buy the next pitcher.

This is where tactics and judgement come into play! As the pitcher is becoming more and more empty, there comes a point where you will have to decide whether the amount you are leaving in the jug is small enough to be finished by the next person. Can you trust your neighbor? Or will he suddenly down the rest of the liquid, leaving you with the bill for the next pitcher!

— BEERHUNTER —

**This classic drinking game is a
simple game for simple people!**

*You will need any amount of players, plus a six-pack
of beer or pop for every four to six players.*

Take all the cans out of their packaging. Choose one
can from every six-pack and shake it vigorously, then
replace it amongst all the others. Depending on your
sense of fair play, you could either mix the cans up so
you don't know which ones are shaken, or you could
keep an eye on the seriously explosive drinking
equipment!

Then simply ask each player to pick a can, any can! This
liquid version of Russian Roulette will lead to much hilarity
as players are dowsed.

— Money in the Kitty —

**A quick game to help buy another
pitcher when you need one in a hurry!**

You will need two to six players, plus three dice.

Each player chooses a number from one to six. They then take it in turns to roll the dice, and each time the dice shows the chosen number of one of the players, that person has to contribute a dollar to the kitty.

For example, there are five players playing, and they've picked the numbers one, two, four, five and six. The first person rolls the dice, and up come three, four and six. Player Four and Player Six each place a dollar in the kitty. There's no Player Three, so that number is ignored. The next person throws the dice and gets one, one and five, so Player One puts two dollars in the kitty and Player Five puts one dollar in the kitty.

And so it carries on, until you're all either out of money, or there's plenty of money to buy the next few rounds to continue playing other drinking games with!

81

— MATING SEASON —

This game is a great opportunity to match-make!

*You will need an even number of players,
plus some pre-prepared 'Mating' cards.*

In advance, prepare some 'Mating' cards in pairs, according to the number of players (see below). Each card represents one part of a mating pair of animals, for example a male and a female cat. Use your imagination for the types of animals included, but do have some fairly ordinary ones in the pack as they are also great fun. Then deal each player one card – give 'male' cards to all the men and 'female' cards to the women – or mix them all up!

Players take alternate man/woman turns to try to find their partners by performing whatever mating ritual they imagine the animal in question normally does to an opposite sex player of their choice. This is great fun to watch even if you've already found your partner – just imagine a male jellyfish searching for his female equivalent! Any player that picks the 'wrong' partner has to pay a drinking forfeit (see p.46). If they still haven't guessed their mate correctly after two tries, the unsuccessful couple both have to finish their drinks as a forfeit.

Examples of 'Mating' card animals:

(A) CAT

(B) DOG

(C) PIG

(D) CHIMPANZEE

(E) GOLDFISH

(F) GORILLA

(G) KANGAROO

(H) ORANG-UTAN

(I) HIPPOPOTAMUS

(J) JELLYFISH.

— GLASSKETBALL —

*Maybe you should invest in some waterproof
clothing before you attempt this game!*

*You will need two players, a referee,
'ball boys' or 'ball girls', a table tennis ball, plus
two full glasses of your chosen drink.*

The objective of this game is to throw the table tennis
ball into your opponent's glass. Both players sit
opposite each other, their legs straight and apart, feet
touching each other's. They both place their full glass
anywhere within the open space thus formed. Once the
glass has been placed, it cannot be moved.

Player One throws the ball, aiming for his opponent's
glass. A successful throw allows him to take a drink and
then have a second throw. If he hits the rim, he is
allowed one more throw – this is where the 'ball boys' or
ball girls' come in handy – they have to retrieve the ball
from wherever it has bounced!

If the player misses his opponent's glass, play passes to the other side. Each successful throw counts as one point, and the winner must be ahead by two clear points to win.

You could, of course, use a golf ball instead of a table tennis ball – it makes for some fantastic splashes! – but beware of breaking the glass in the process!

— ENDURANCE —

This 'game' could also be called 'Bursting Bladder' – for reasons that will soon become painfully clear!

You will need any amount of players, a referee, plus a stopwatch.

The rules of this game are extremely simple…but the results are very uncomfortable!

Everyone sits in a room. The referee has a stopwatch and announces every full minute, *"DRINK"*, upon which everyone in the room has to take a large (and the emphasis is on **large**) gulp of their drink. After another minute, he again says *"DRINK"*, and another gulp has to be taken. This carries on and on and on!

Eventually the first person gives up and leaves the room to go to the bathroom! They are immediately put out of the game and everyone else carries on. The next person will leave shortly thereafter. Ultimately, there will only be one player left and he is the winner…or is he?

LAGOON WEB SITE

Games, Books, Puzzles and Gizmos

Visit the Lagoon Web Site to view a
staggering range of fantastic games,
puzzles and books to suit all.

www.lagoongames.com

OTHER TITLES IN THE SERIES

The Ultimate Late Night Party Games Collection
ISBN: 1–902813–29–4

The Ultimate Travel Games Collection
ISBN: 1–902813–30–8

The Ultimate After Dinner Games Collection
ISBN: 1–902813–28–6

OTHER TITLES BY LAGOON BOOKS

KIDS MAZE PUZZLE BOOKS

Wanda the Witch and the Magical Maze
(1–902813–11–1)

Dr CK Fortune and the Lost City Labyrinth
(1–902813–12–X)

BRAIN-BOOSTING PUZZLE BOOKS

Brain-Boosting Cryptic Puzzles
(1–902813–21–9)

Brain-Boosting Visual Logic Puzzles
(1–902813–20–0)

Brain-Boosting Lateral Thinking Puzzles
(1–902813–22–7)